Bewick Walks To Scotland

Sally Evans

Sally Evans
to Myles — Gaelic poet
friend
March 04

ARROWHEAD
PRESS

First published 2004 by:
Arrowhead Press
70 Clifton Road, Darlington,
County Durham, DL1 5DX
Tel: (01325) 260741

Typeset in 11pt Bembo by
Arrowhead Press

Email: editor@arrowheadpress.co.uk
Website: http://www.arrowheadpress.co.uk

Arrowhead Press acknowledges the financial assistance of
Arts Council England, North East

Printed by Athenaeum Press, Gateshead.

*To Watty
who travelled to Carlisle
in search of a place*

Acknowledgements

The publisher thanks the President and Secretary of The Bewick Society for their assistance in gathering source material for this book, and the staff at National Trust Cherryburn for their cheerful and helpful responses to what may have seemed silly questions at the time of his visit.

Versions of some of the poems in this book have previously appeared in the following publications:

Magazines:

Second Light, Envoi, Zed2O, Iron Magazine, Northwords, Chapman, Poetry Cornwall, The Herald, New Writing Scotland, The Red Wheelbarrow, Nomad, Scotia Review.

Anthologies:

Things Not Seen, Brigflatts Visited, The Watergaw, Edinburgh: an intimate city.

Contents

Bewick walks to Scotland

Further poems

Bewick walks to Scotland

In 1776, Thomas Bewick, the engraver, then aged 23, took a two month walking tour from Cherryburn, his home near Newcastle. Starting on "a hot day in June", and carrying only a few pounds, he went through Northumberland, Cumberland, the borders, lowlands, and West central highlands of Scotland, returning from Leith to South Shields by boat, and arriving back in Newcastle on 12th August. Bewick briefly outlined this adventure in his memoir written in 1822.

Skylark

The illustrations in this section are wood engravings by Thomas Bewick (1753-1828).

Newcastle

Here are my drawings and paintings of birds,
stored sheaves under the workbench, propped
behind casket or candlestick. I never stopped
adding to my notes, colours rather than words.
You see they are creased, I used them as templates.
Often would I stare at the blank horizon,
a carefully folded sheet in my grip,
as my mind took off, perhaps some quip
of Cunningham's ringing rhyme in my brain,
skylarks carolling upward in dry air
or quick hares starting sideways in confusion.
From Kenton or from Carter Bar,
from Cheviot, could I contemplate
a Scottish range to North or West
or both the Irish and the German main?
I was gated by hedged starry footpaths,
sea-coasts and meadows were mine
and westerly Wylam, wildlifed seclusion,
the quiet of cottaged reaches of the Tyne.

Before I drew for business or delight
or learned here or in London town my trade,
engraving on wood and copper, letters, blocks,
flourishes, cressets churches might desire
or august corporations fancy,
Ralph Beilby training me in technique,
my brother following me in my learning,
I, as a country-knowledgeable lad
who looked to every teacher with the need
of finding peak or slope or grandstand,
a way of looking from a visionary day,

an answer without question, burning, once
touching the surface of our empirical clay,
our geological not theological empire,
I left my nursery and walked to Scotland.

Blackbird

We knew, we knew, exalted Nature
and lauded Science held truth and glory.
We challenged those besotted fools
of counties palatine or graded schools
or courtly finery. We had found coal
with fossil ferns, saw their significance.
We had held traffic from the Tyne
with Holland, the Enlightenment, from Leith
and Cherbourg of the Auld Alliance;
we knew of Jutland and of Denmark;
our local language flowed towards Oslo;
and Birmingham and London fed from us,
oh yes, depended on us, old Newcastle.

That stuffy buffer, my future self
(if not, there'll be no denial)
leaves gaps in his guesswork here,
supposing the young man austere,
reflecting an elder, a young blond pilgrim
he calculates will appear.
The narrative's incomplete.
I cannot recount my life
in a regular series of I-sentences.
All I have to say I have figured.
By circumstance and chances triggered,
my craftsman hand, so attuned to the pen,
relies on moments, not the words for them.

In trying to tell you what it was like,
circling in Scotland, a headlong hike,
in my knowledgeless and youth-ful state,
I must speak from the young man, not from the old
nor from the busy cutter of a fast selling line
of book illustrations. It is the draftsman
in the making that I am, not yet the draftsman.

Haltwhistle

Not Newcastle's invader
but borderers, farmers and worse,
further over the fells than I ever walked
seeking the small, gentle things of the countryside.
I still found the gentle things, wild roses
gooseberries and redcurrants in the hedge
round each earth-hump trying to be a field
in that squashed, crossed, upheaving country;
rills running innocently into the South Tyne,
where, those bone-white fortifications
hiking high on the line of sight,
abandoned military ruins ruin the view.
Everything tries to ingnore the past,
but it is there, like a carcass in the marsh,
or a skeleton blown in the treeless wind.

Here were the corbies at a gate.
My cousin lives here, out in the wilds.
He is a prize fighter. He needs to be.
He guided me round rather nasty hovels,
operations to scavenge the military stone.
Not to mention the sheep-stealing.
To be mixed up in that business
is not at all advised.
Wild stories run down to Newcastle
with the floodwaters, refugees
fiddle and play their way through Hexham
down to the work and wheat of docksides.
There was an ash tree, there a pine.
I have followed a footpath all this time

and it leads to a peat hole,
a sodding peat hole
at the back of beyond
and I must retrace my many steps.

Snipe

Brampton

A country there was no room for
compressed into a town
of sophisicated music,
the magic violin –
where Scottish spirit
and English craftsmanship
collide, give life to
a box that wants to sing,
wood that trembles
as these deciduous hills.
I feel the country change, law change.
Language, as always, is debatable.

Carlisle

Grim gate-holder
of wispy hinterland,
down from bower of brigand
round the quicksanded coast,
dangerous estuaries
some know the paths across,
capital of lost valleys
and secret ports:
here we refill our glass:
Here, in old hostelries
in the town's shadows
a jar, a jostle, a jest:
their business to know who I am.
What? Yes he is my cousin. Famous? Him?
That backwoodsman, no-man's-lander,
a fighter. Why aye, man.

Langham

I hope the road will follow this river's
wooded otter pools.
More farms, less lonely, cluster,
scattered chickens round their doors.
I suppose this is my first Scottish water,
diffidently snaking down the hill,
wide enough to ruffle with the breezes
and very good to drink.
How late the bluebells flower!
How the hidden ramsons stink,
creeping up a wooded creek.
A plover calls from fields, a raucous crow
flaps out of trees along the river,
a makeshift portent.
You can imitate its cry in words.
I cannot draw its cry in the river sand.
Neither can I depict the whiff
from the ramsons carpet, nor can wordsmith.

I know that Edinburgh is north-east.
I've introductions there.
I wonder if it can compare
with fabulous Durham's cliff?
I'm told that Edinburgh's wider.
Tomorrow, or the next day, I'll be there
but now wet sky and wetter land
lie on my route,
spread out on either hand.

Starling

Stow road from Galashiels

The road winds, ambling round the trees,
at gradient and pace to please
a peaceful cuddy with a cart
of worsted for the city's heart.
These overgrown fat lambs carouse
on tilthy pastures, unaware
how blood and bones were wasted there
in all this land, a shire's length square
while border brother fought with brother,
thinking himself Scot, Northron, or some other.

I am meant to be an artist of peace.
I could never be an artist of war.
There was one self-hanged man I saw –
I was never more sorrowful,
before or after,
than over that eyeful
dangling beside a brook.
Someone's troubles are over,
humanity toils on.
Skip on, skip on, canny lamb,
before I eat a plate of your cousin.

The Hare

Edinburgh

Here is Edinburgh.
Here are its nearer hills
I have been seeking.
It looks as though
the whole of Scotland has arrived here too.
My Inn has proved expensive and unnerving:
tankards and platters much too massive.
I scarpered.
Then, in the sackcloth city
I found one after my own heart,
a student of the engraver's art
who led me round, unlocking
tales and sights my foreignness was blocking.

The Academy! The University!
The colleges! The kirk!
The courts! The institutions!
I wondered if we had passed any writers,
hot-footing it from library to desk
or from stanza to stationer.
I dare not think of the schooling it would take
to write like the philosophers and poets,
reading, understanding, memorising!
I cannot write, but I can draw,
paint and sketch, can make a pen
respond to my cajoling.

Glasgow

Met up in Glasgow's urban commonroom
with more from the apprentice network,
Geordie and Scots intelligible one to the other,
and Glasgow, like a larger Sunderland,
creeping round its nursling river –
less of a horse-pond than the Wear or Tyne.
Here come ribaldry and rhyme,
beerslopping through the door of the hostelry,
Sauchiehall Street pie jokes, rural horrors,
the debunking of modest lasses. But my art
is my mistress, much more demanding
in that I have not satisfied her yet.
I watch her, every whim and curio.
When I become an impresario,
old master of art whom the world may forget,
remember, or pigeonhole (it matters not)
she will still be my mistress, though I hide
her like a dowager in imagined pride.

Goldfinch

Jay

Lomond

The road past Lomond is peopled.
I have stood on Tynemouth's rock
to watch the shipping river meet the sea
steepled and crowned by topmast and cliffhead,
to vote the Tyne the greatest waterscape.
I now accept the wide, cool rivalry
of my first vision of Scotland's southerly loch,
as I plod its western, popularised track
and I am aware of my smallness in its face.
I do not seem superior to the birds
I recognise from youthful studiousness,
indeed, they have wings, they are more, we less
who trudge two-legged, cross streams,
flagged marshes, crags. Our ingenuity
which seems so ingenious, is not much use
outside our normal flat page of etching.
At the end of knowledge the world might well be flat.
We fall off it as surely as if it were.
So, this outlook on Lomond
and that view of the Tyne, are two woodblocks.
They cannot be put together or compared,
in the multiple universe in which they occur.
One will tailpiece a book of butterflies.
One will gaze out of a gazetteer.

Killin Bridge

Rocks in the torrent under the trees
are linked by a stunning bridge
distracting the eye from the Dochart.
Pines, Caledonian Pines
and leaf, flowerlet and island
surround the glassy slabs
of moving water. Under the slopes
the township moves. Pearlers
slink round the river checking mussels.
Drovers and carriers head for the bridge.
I duck in a deuk. A whinnying horse
crosses to where he knows there'll be rest,
bringing his western load to the mill.

Osprey

Stag

The Stag

A trail under the trees
near Loch Katrine
and all is silent, barring
a bird, a wind-sigh.
God's creation rises
in the form of a great stag
his magnificent branchy horns and head
alert under an oak-copse
as he steps into the sun
ten feet away from me
as though he were an oak tree come to life.
No, do not turn and run.
A pagan revelation,
personification of beauty –
I need this vision. When it is my duty
to sketch him from memory,
or from tame, toned-down specimen,
I shall draw on this meeting.
I am with him in the wild.

Dark Road

A moonless time
I have wandered so long!
In darkness, I perceive
movement and sound on the road in front of me.
The track bends under trees.
I lift my hawthorn stick
and stand aside. Perhaps the animal
will pass in ignorance that I am here.
A too-close snuffle.
"Whoa", I bawl quietly, prodding the air.
The deer objects. He rushes me.
I wriggle from his shoulder,
shield my head from his horns,
run, and he is gone.

Quiet again.
Another too-close scuffle.
"Scram", I bawl, not so quietly,
prodding the air, and catching soft resistance.
The farm hand jumps and runs.
I hear him swear. I call,
"Sorry, mate, I thought you were a deer".

Loch Tay

I roamed hills mad, wild as a wildcat,
reasonless, driven by survival instinct, as he,
and with equal disdain for the dull —
but my queens lurking beyond the glades
were box–slivers touched by cutting blades.
In a summer as long and light as any
I roamed as lordly as any bull,
as curious as otters, I was animal and man.
I saw rabbits washing their ears, angry cuddies
kicking, cantering, sailing over five foot walls
to prove their prowess; muttering old men,
dumb shepherds, drunken shepherds,
chicken yards, doves and ravens, tickled fish,
oats with scarecrows, rank and outlandish
shallow stone slopes eaten down
to the fernshoots, greyling grouped in muddy ponds,
stagnant copses huddled below the exposure line
and vast howling mountains, tunes
played on them by the voiceless thumbs of breezes.
I led my herd of ability and hope,
abstract and unconvincing, up each slope,
and met a spirit sheltering in a cave
from a thunderstorm the sky's anvil gave me,
sound to sear me, light to save me.

Highland farm

The girl ran like a deer. I had kissed her.
It was my doing. No practice, no finesse.
No wonder the wild thing, surprised
raced for the hill from my grasp.
I must go on, let it pass. In my clumsy way
I tried to express my appreciation,
but my vision has this flaw, it is artistic.
That wild beauty on legs, those eyes' creation
in unfamed wilderness, eagle and sheep
siblings and trout, hayrick and dogs,
are her society. Be realistic,
she awaits a young shepherd from over the hill,
for his voice to break, for his height to grow,
till he can pull over the screes in all elements,
to prise her from her parents in snow, mist and winter
or in spring with the bluebell, the laverock.

Curlew

Tyndrum

My pennies and halfpence are going far.
Hospitality is greater the more severe
the conditions folk live in. Language has failed.
Over a border of our vernacular
to the Gaelic of age and renown, I stammer.
My language is no more than myself, my open face.
I am weak in my walking alone. I am strong
because I dare be alone, because I willed to come.
Here is a long plain, vast and veiled
by the time it takes to traverse.
Will our north England engineers invent locomotion
to outstrip a horse? A ludicrous notion!

Walking, I wonder, if I had a violin
would the isolate farmers welcome and take me in?
How, more than at present? They give,
and I cannot pay, only my purse's pence,
which they will not take, waving away,
cancelling favour with bannocks
as though unneeding of munificence.
More, they need luck, from the gods and strangers.
I sketch in the sand with sharp rocks,
intriguing their unlettered children.

Orchy

I spent all day at home at a waterfall,
crawled to the overhang, swam the deep pool,
watched boiling cold water, a phenomenon,
measuring in mind the tilt of the ledge
where water slides down, glass then foam,
a swirling current, pulled by gravity
to most un-grave result. The water is stunned
but happy. It is. I'll draw breakers
against beach or breakwater many times,
trying to translate into line-shape their persistent din.
The chortling sound of a river falling, gliding
smoothly and slowly with the waterlevel,
produces awe. All evening I drink it in.

Water Rail

Return to Stirling

Without an eye for the land
I would soon be in danger –
not from wolves, for they have gone –
I should like to have seen one.
Nor from the utterly shy
wild martens and cats
but from the land itself,
boggy and ridged under heather,
furrowed under the fern.
I have come so far, yet some days
a dozen miles is far.
I think I have been near Inveraray.
But there was no road
because I was in the wild country
and I stayed in the wild country
because there was no road.

So I followed rills of water
but they tumbled too steep.
I crossed the flanks of mountains
keeping below their peaks.
I let the loch come nearer,
or the sea stay on my right
but I let luck guide me
and she did so, as I walked
and as I slept through each short night.

Now, in August, the nights begin
to lengthen, darkness has time to cool
and I head back to the east,
to find the lowlands and resume
my normal role.
It takes me longer than I thought.
At last I am on a road
to Stirling. Past loch after loch
I trek, suddenly dreadfully tired

and suddenly I crave Newcastle,
Quayside, Barras Bridge,
the cherry trees on chares,
with almost overpowering longing.
What, not Stirling yet?
Callander and old Doune –
then Stirling's castle's visible
and at last my feet complain –
the road is hard.
And can I get a bed?
With difficulty –
the same goes for a bite of supper.

Leith to Shields, by boat

Heaven preserve me, barely twenty-three
and my first ship voyage will be my last
whether or not I live to record the life
I know recording is my work in. Youth's tour
over the very best the country offers, solitude,
natural sights and scenery, hospitality,
understanding and fellowship – wiser than war is wine –
finds severe and unexpected danger.
A coaster of 26 souls in a storm –
souls sick and unattractive in a small confine,
we are pitched, tossed, upturned for three days.

A respite in the weather brings a shaft
of calm light swell near Lindisfarne –
great heavens, we are the wrong side of the island
and nearly grounded in its sands. We tack back
away from the sandbanks studded with wrecked carts
and make it round the channel.
Now we shall live, set shaken foot on land,
now we make sail, well north of Tyneside.
I watch the coastline, cleared of cloud, depart,
dazzled by resurrected gleams from Chillingham Moor
overpowering the wilderness in Cheviot's plain.

Chillingham

I had heard of the white wild cattle there.
Later I was to depict a bull
both great and gentle, magnificent
yet vulnerable, for the Esquire
who hoped my miniature might equal
that bestial, genial might. I'd hide behind a wall,
near to a bolting-tree, should that young bull
decide not to accept my homage –
it would be a big woodblock, liable to crack,
but then it was to be one print only.
Until light can do its own etching
the gentry will always be fetching me.

Wild Cattle

Land

Home! home! to Bewick's town,
Bewick's country, hedges grown
round folds of meadow, rivers, rides.
How is happiness mine to approach
when the known map is such a mess?
Paris inviting turmoil, Eastern steppes in thrall,
fighting beginning for diamonds and gold.
There is so much under our feet! The black diamonds
of coal to kill for, Whitby's coastal jet,
rustless metal and smoothest rock in halls
deep below, or cropping, crystal gems.
I do not make jewelled pumpkin or coach
beautiful with the possession of peasants.
I ennoble Cinderella by simply lining
her rich beauty that needs no adorning.
I can make Goldilocks and her cuddly animals
sleep forever wakeable on a folded page.
I make a levelling using science and knowledge.
The scientists of Newcastle and Birmingham
cry Technology Saves, and preach
presentable, confident sermons in stones
to a wholly approving college.

A softening of the sky. The road from Shields
switchbacks through Gateshead to my river.
Unlike marauding soldiers, I deliver.
Now I come to my own – now I return
for this is Bewick's country, the hawthorn hedge
spilling holly, palisaded environments
around woods, fields and trees, the companions
to old grey walls, retired from defending
the red Dutch tiles of Newcastle.
The life and wildlife, hinterland of the Tyne,
quaysides and markets, mansions and orchards

distant, and better so, here at Cherryburn,
this shall be yours, for it is mine.

London, York, I will visit, in London work
but here shall I belong, in my life that is begun,
here shall blocks tumble on my workbenches,
here shall lettering and leafage sprout,
the young and old of dog and rabbit,
stag, bird, cat and homo sapiens.
My brothers, playmates, their every caper
and what they are about,
printed, repeatedly, on paper, rags
from these black blocks,
coal, wood, beech, box,
till fifty years have sped like one,
and I, an old man, now attempt, in creaky words,
a rough recounting of my memoir, knowing
I shared in an age of watching knowledge grow,
be it dicky-birds or the travellers' reports
of jungle cats. I knew the world was so.
I learned to think the wildcats' thoughts
and those of waterbirds and stags.

In this strong north England city
I look to my neighbours the Scots
to their wildlife and my own youth,
to their future geologists, engineers
and scientists who will develop
our new observancy
and carry on our work,
we who are artists and scientists,
who make a go of our lives
in the places we love.

I make no apology, give you only
white spaces in black
till the warbler or cur,
cliff-face or galleon,
farm-woman or fox,
by my steady hand studied,
leap again from my blocks.

North Pennine Accent

I am constantly told
I have an English accent.
It is from the North
Pennines – Teesdale, Lonsdale,
where brown rivers ripple
over sharp consonants,
every vowel whole,
thee earth, thee oak, thee apple
clothing woodlands,
travelling
a pleasurable dactyl,
discovery staccato,
understanding
four long slow sounds,
the sympathy of the outsider
legendary, independence
a thoughtful peal
of distant village bells.

It is good to carry
these memories in my tongue,
one landscape my background
to another spectacular one –
where I and my unchanging race
are settled – slopes of trees
deciduous, wakening, infused
by horizontal sunbeams
to grey, gold, russet, sage
and lime – the calls
of animals and named birds –
cuckoo sung home,
evening swallows with an
African accent.
And when the deer

dance up the hill, the stag
(who does not know he is Scottish)
speaks rarely and perfectly.

Yes my friends
I have an English accent
and yet I know your grammar
and varying accents
distinct in moments
as only a wanderer can,
who knows what to look for
alongside the rivers
that flow from your forests
in all of their details,
diffusing the dangerous
brightness of the sun.

On my youth, mis-spent in the Lake District

On Cat Bells in snow above a mirror-
lake of stony slate, or pinnacling
the sharp chipped axeblade of Striding Edge,
or sauntering back down Helvellyn
and thinking, It's you next week, Scafell,
oriented always by the Langdale Pikes,
compass-pulled to the base at Dungeon Ghyll
and being beaten by my brother over
the number of times OldMan Coniston
had ridden under our walking boots –
lovingly dubbined for the next expedition,
the next privileged middleclass student weekend
or the next vacation hamfistedly serving
in a Windermere restaurant by evening
to be up in the fells again, mountain-minded
in mistless eaarliest morning: to smile
benignly on the canoeists, sailors, tentsmen,
even the roped-up rockface scalers,
to follow those holy paths in the shorn grass
up to the peaks and ridges
away from our flatter northern villages
to the birds' eye, god's eye, poet's ear views
was worth missing the swinging cities for
and all social penance remembering.

Autumn in the Lakes

De Quincey's coming from Edinburgh in his old mini
he ought to change that car, it won't take
the speeds on the new road past Carlisle
they've finished it now there are plain-clothes cop cars
looking out for the likes of De Quincey
perhaps that's where he is
explaining to the Keswick lot
that he's due on at Lake Lit
and that was his reason for speeding.
He'd use his best French.
Talking of Carlisle yes *Carlyle*
sent us a salutation of encouragement to the participants
R. Burns (deceased) refused the invitation
way back in January.
By the way Coleridge where's the subscription list?
Why isn't there one?
Well there'll be the Mayor of Grasmere
the Lord High Chancellor of Loughrigg
the party from the All Lake District Hospital
Long Term Therapy Unit
what's that Dorothy
the trees are wonderful this time of year?

41

The Gardener Listening to Eroica

Copper leaves, darker than holy wells,
spin down from soundproof trees
where daisies burn the contour of the slope.
Indoors, amid cool corridors
a gardener listens to *Eroica*.

Late outside, he is copper leaves
darker than holy wells.
He has given over gardening, listens
from his narrow shed, in the space
by the great purple tree.

Blank Pages

Nothing was written on my two blank pages
blown away by the wind
but they were precious,
I did not realise how precious
until they were blown away by the wind.

The blank white page is not an enemy
to the poet, it is a friend,
a friend to all for whom words are stars
shining, unconnected
until with an unexpected line

shown by the wave of a tree branch,
an arrow, dart of the eye of mind,
the eddy, direction, the drift of wind
bringing that linking thought of words
that will expand to fill blank paper

like a constellation of snatched stars
from an empty universe
that did not appreciate darkness
until bereaved of it
by creation.

Basil's land

The gentle northern tongue
travel took not from me,
the Scots would not look on,
Southrons would sing wrong,
I heard in tree and dale,
beck and fell,
but only one
who used the sound well,
where Yorkshire is south,
Stainmore the backbone,
opened his mouth,
made notes drip from stone
where high on the fell
a windswept tree looked out,
saw the scars of the sea,
forces, an estuary,
in his own land only
Northern mid-light,
a vocabulary of vision,
solitude, delight.

In the Country

The castle has gone
from the sides of the river,
it cannot be replaced.
Caressed by wind and rain
and buffeted by storm
the castle has gone
from the sides of the river.

A language has gone
from the sides of the river,
unvisited by people
a language has gone
and cannot be replaced.
It has gone utterly
from the sides of the river.

The castle demolished,
the language dismantled.
Yet the river, the river,
that sends down its water
from the clouds of its sources
and rills in its stretches,
still flows and remains.

Flashes

Slithery, watery fur slick
under a peopled bridge –

I recognise you from a score
of poems about otters

by poets, like me, who care
that they're naturalists.

Who's going to believe
how you glisten and plop

as you navigate the bridge,
skim through the reeds,

the drainage cut, and away
from the three anglers

and two courting couples
none of whom notice you?

Your whereabouts I'll keep
a secret to save

you from the haters
of anarchist fish eaters.

Otter! What next?
Me, with a quicksilver text.

That which cannot be seen
and cannot be spoken of

except in flashes.

Blind Man by the River

For fifty years he has touched base here,
stepping through the valley he knows perfectly,
tree by oak-trunk or root-railing,
topsoil waterlogged under the grass,
autumn drakes fighting and flailing
as the leaf-bringing gale subsides.

He knows exactly what it is like.
The sounds tie in with his pictures.
The river, rising and falling like his own life,
whispers its metric philosophy,
swishing round the fox-trails into the dog-roses,
instantly sensitive to rainfall in the hills.

He blends with the varied pathways along the banks,
moves in their half-shade, disperses mists.
He tastes the articulate water on his fingertips.
He blinks, and the water is sharp black and white.
Pausing at the seat, facing down-river,
the cuckoo's gone, he hears the woodpecker.

Having lost his sight but not his vision
he dreams through time, translating the riverside
into its paraphrased reworded epic,
ever-running, actors and extras squirrelling
and gliding, a confluence long ago begun
of gleaming stanzas set to the evening sun.

Farewell

The week before we left our other house
one visited our garden. On the branch
across the window where the sparrows,
robin and bluetit had come regularly
throughout our sojourn there, on this one day
the bright fire of a goldfinch burned. He came,
he would have spoken if he knew our language,
and then he went. Apparently at times
the goldfinch does a circuit of an area,
checking out rowan or cotoneaster,
– no doubt that was it. We had been thinking
perhaps our birds would notice when we'd gone
and soon we went, with memories of the garden
and the goldfinch we had seen just once.

Winter

The summer visitor
never sees the winter white,
never sees mountains light
against a stone-grey sky
solidly towering,
sees no snowflakes flowering
nor the drifts
falling against their poles
or the black salted road
relentless, rolling
emptily north or south.

But when the summer visitor stays
the nights give their secrets,
the winter its solace,
the grey and white mountains
something to understand,
something to climb,
in time, traced by snow-flurries.

The fused sound and mind
that drives poems pageward
produces its crystals
formed from the cold,

Rope-strong words
that hold with the whisky,
squalour or valour,
gleaming and glamour,
hardship, the leaden
feast and the berry
and feather of winter
forever, once ever
that first darkness is shared.

Fireside

How flames rise from the wood:
a shy lick of forked tongue
appears and vanishes
into that cavern of dream,
and embers sing their song.

The cat with her soft fur
and calm exterior
watches them flicker: she
shares magic with the flames
and keeps their secrets. We

sit awed, for we remember
how life began that way,
quietly watching heat
glow out of wood and peat,
and how their abstract art

was all the human heart
had need of, while their power
expands into a flower,
then drops and fades to ashes.
Fire is what we will:

it links us with the dead,
who sat much as we sit,
and said much as we said.
Its moments of delight
are here today, tonight,

and spell the future. Flames
are more worth watching than
the road or television.
Peace wakes the cat; she washes.
The logs assert their charm.

Music and snowflakes

A long road into whiteout, homeward drivers
at careful distances maintain low speed
steadily over accumulating snow,
among dark hedges and roadside trees,
alluring pitfalls of fairyland,
our rural trails' harsh soft extremities.
Each in our own world grip lone wheel,
view the wide whirling from tense seat.
A concert steals out from the radio,
deceives, seems scripted for the ride.
In trapped concentration we listen.
A wide symphony of snowflakes glide,
dance in their darkness to this one piece.
Minutes and miles match music's phrases,
till each turns singly at lane or gate
and I abandon the composer last
where notes still flurry from the solitude
of some long forgotten, alien
shared sparse journey of danger.

Winter, above Amulree

No deer to be seen –
the first soft snow
decidedly drifting down,
sitka spruce transformed
to green-white ghosts,
the heather dusted,
the roads a slithering floor
for their revelry,
the black tracks of tyres
ribboning them, two cars
anxious to escape
before the white-out deepens
and with the snow, a firm
cold temperature, above ice
but flat, unbroken cold.

Snow above Amulree,
the first snow of the year,
the high moor settling
to hibernate all winter,
January, February,
snug in the snow's white hold,
below the long-blown winds
and soaring gales –
roads to rest, white trails
in silence from motors –
the solitary tramp
of a hardy countryman –
then at last, queues of deer
coming down, coming down
to the truce of the skyline,
from black wastes of winter.

Snow and Deer, Dalwhinnie

under the swoop of snow
are roots to feed you;

under the ice the burns cascade;

darkness harries the sky;
the hillside whitens;

your heads are lowered against the wind;

and you wait for the storms to go
over the mountain tops.

White Cattle

The white bull stood on Chillingham moor
stubborn as the season Bewick prowled
behind the tree that seeded those boughs,
graving the white bull's ancestor.
In the night's isolation and gloaming
the ancient herd here roamed.

No A1 then, no motorway, no estate wall,
no paygate gawpers. Only a roughshod visionary,
the eighteenth-century safety of a tree
and the uncompromising snow-laden moor,
across the slush, potholes, horseshit, the roar
and paraphernalia of dark farmlands.

Mild, patient, beautiful as legends,
two young males, milk-white, curly,
their muzzles black matt thorn hedges
outlined by Northumberland snow,
their eyes dark bright borderland wells
drawn from prehistory.

Unruffled, straight-backed, horns hefty,
they gaze from christmassy straw
at a picture window of palings, the high wall
risen from their wintry country,
and they confront me on their trail,
rewarding as a brace of unicorns.

Meeting the Ploughman

He has ploughed nine acres and no-one notices.
The black field curls round the black wood,
crested by seagulls and a crow.
No snowdrops; nothing but is desolate.
I walk up the strip by the field's edge,
cutting a path across seasons, days and years,
plough upon olden plough, ear upon ear of wheat.
His striking blade has made me too aware
of desolation, flowering, birth, defeat,
isolate thousand who have walked as I.
He has observed on turning steady time
the nine brooding loquacious acres
alive and dead, or served and beaten-down,
ocean of fishing-birds, sky of worm,
path of passer-by, clock of the living,
larder of the surviving. He has ploughed
tremendous meagre acres, where my path
treks up and down, faces I did not see,
hoot of the owl in the wood and the land's ghost,
rhyme of the tractor-wheels, burden of hoof,
the foot, the eye, back working, shoulder, yoke,
the tractor seat, fibreglass sides and roof
through which the rain that touches my long hair
and warms the soil's fresh ramps, spits to warn
the ploughman of reverberating grandeur,
slithering fear.
                    A woman passes by
a hedge all twigs and bramble-skeletons,
and pauses, courteous or exhausted where the view
breathes to itself

and takes flight down the hill.

Young American walking the coastline

There he was, at the campsite breakfast,
the young American walking the coastline,
pack and boots, jeans and cap,
eating his toast before the day's lap
of cliff, coast, road and beach.

The warden, between fixing eggburgers
on a spitting stove at the bar,
asked him how many weeks last year
it had taken to trail the seascapes –
for this was his second trek, via Thurso
to Ayrshire from Inverness.

Yes, we smiled, we're from Scotland,
from Edinburgh, yes, it's nice,
but the tourists go round the castle, not us –
we don't walk the coastline twice.
We caught sight of him, tiny and grand
as we sped past on the coast road,

wondering, confusingly, whether it's best
to walk round Scotland from East or West,
whether set to the morning or evening sun.
You never know what an American will do next,
we added, thinking all morning of this young man,

as he piled Scotland into his rucksack,
his face as weathered as the rocks
mesmerised by the forest,
a captive of the open shore,
pacing the uncontrollable headlands
and racing the unbeatable sun.

Motorway with owl and geese

A motorway overwhelmed at dawn
by thousands of geese unwinding their skeins

on fields of translucent white, tea-leaves
to stir a storm, doodlebugs thudding

on pilgrimages to Ireland and Mourne
whose wings beat three feet

above the warned wave of cobles
coasting the migrating morning

of international geese, where our dawn
crosses under theirs.

A day on, our southward return
against the enticing rhythmic moon

setting a pace for language in its field-wise face
and the swing of strong wings –

the white owl lobs through the darkness,
past cars' predictable pale darts

correcting the motorway's passive, unattended
calendar, its clock of ghosts.

Arrivals

Swallows are home at the many eaved inn
at a country lane-end in summer.

It is impossible not to invent their gladness to be home
as they check their corners,
visit the sparrows, swoop over buttercups,

impossible not to notice them caulking nest-cracks with
mud
collected with fluttering grace from the field-path,

impossible not to believe in their jubilant triumph
at the forthcoming miniature faces
peeping over the rim of their nests,

impossible not to try to imagine
what it has felt like, the flight from Africa
for the beautiful, able, intelligent swallows
it is not possible to follow.

Through the silence

Muffled yaffle through the silence
drumdrumdrumdrumdrum

Tall close trees mottled with lichen
in the cleanest air,
dry, cool evening, pale white sky
quiet pathway, none
but my companion and I
passing by

drumdrumdrumdrumdrum again
– silence even deeper –

We look upward, crane our necks
you are safely hidden
Bewick said your young will run
up and down trunks before they fly
but no such sight for us
not in front of us do you

drumdrumdrumdrumdrumdrumdrum
drumdrumdrumdrumdrum.

Don't you ever bother singing?
Need you, with the small wood ringing
drumdrumdrumdrumdrumdrumdrum

Silence springs back into place
like a branch you flew away from.
In the gaps between your sound
we hear profound seclusion
in your haunt.

Free verse crow

Suddenly there's a gift.
A tame crow.
Padding in the garden.
Looking at me wisely.
Doesn't fly away.

Unexpected, like a gift.
Surprising, like a gift.
Never had one
just like that before.

Grey round the head.
Clean, dark. Down
to earth, and doesn't
seem to want anything,

as he loiters on the green
companionable grass.

He's a free verse crow.

Real Thistles

*(On Les Murray having remarked
that he couldnt find any thistles in Scotland)*

You'd have found your thistles
on motorway shoulders, in the cracks
beside barns, in small time gardens
and other town yards, and you'd have
known them from our yarns,
stamped in gold on book spines.

Cracked into crystal whisky-
tumblers they soothe the inebriated
ditches, or still adorn allotments'
protesting potato trenches,
or crouch rough beside rivers.
They are banished from farms.

Fact: they are a notifiable
invasive weed: if your neighbour
lets thistle seed, you can cop him.
He must poison them or dig them up.
But they flower unstoppably in our minds,
defiant beauty in unkempt lands.

Artificial Grass

The light opening out after winter
I step round the meandering park
to see if they have planted snowdrops.
Someone's been at work — crocus leaves.
Oak saplings bigger than Annie's,
under the grey centennial trees.
Bright gulls face the wind, as always,
pattern-repeats covering acres.
A fenced-in training ground,
full football pitch, has suddenly gone green —
it looks like thick moss on concrete.

Among the oak-leaves, at the edge
I reach my fingers down — harsh plastic!
Artificial grass! It bamboozles
oak-leaves, twigs and debris — looks realistic.
I'd like to make its perpetrators a few million
artificial oak-leaves to go with it — from real
ecological woodpulp. Or perhaps it'd be better —
undulating tinder — if I made them out of words.

Translation of a Non-Existent Gaelic Poem

It was not in my expectation
that you would understand this poem,
so here is the English:
it will not speak in your sentiments
nor sing in your heart,
for it is not the full shilling,
only broken and bruised
will it hope to utter the words themselves,
roan and yellow flowers
on the dappled floor of the woods
of the dictionaries,
the bright coin of its imagery
glinting in dark hollows
where the huntsmen crooned their lament
to the four winds of meaning.

The poem fluttered past
when you were not looking for it,
because it was you yourself
that was fishing in the water for it,
it was you I saw in your boat
anchored among the rocks
where my words might be shipwrecked,
waterlogged shoals of song
off the island's lee.

It was in my expectation
you would listen to my poem's music,
that is why I wrote the bloody thing,
striving in my workshop
with quern, loom and distaff –
trying to make some sense
of those old-fashioned implements,
and it was to you I sent the e-mail

from my croft, when the postman
couldn't get through the snowdrifts,
but I run my computer off the generator,
so I can get my poems down to you
in Edinburgh or Glasgow
before I have even written them,

before I have ventured out
across the hill of experience
in the quest for the poem's ending
so difficult of attainment –
as I sit here by my fireside
finishing my dram and my dream.

Greetings to Cornwall

Ringed inland by my rim of hills
I am about as far away
as it is possible to drive in a day,
but the email almost instantly
sets off down the country, faster
than the autumn swallows
as they head for light and warmth,
faster than the moon sinks south,
the storm-thrown clouds
or my thoughts themselves, scudding
from northern forest to southern shore,
mountain village to quay andbeach,
riverside to ocean's edge.

An old, grey, fissured telegraph pole
stands in the thick hedge of my garden.
Loopy oldfashioned wires reach round
over our heads to my nine neighbours
(an English maypole all gone wrong).
Our ravaged rowan tree, the half that is left,
the guardian of my Scottish ground
shoots up new immortal leaflets
through converging wires
and gives its power to all my emails
as with this measured message I send
greetings to Cornwall from Scotland.

Cow-parsley

Once I missed the school bus, walked
lanes of cow-parsley on the winding road
connecting the village to the world.
Afterwards, the bus was optional.

Day after spellbound day I am walking
through the memorial cow-parsley
where I have scented too much travelling
ever to retrace that lazy Rubicon.

Ullapool

You know you're in Ullapool
when the little town is a sea town,
lorries roll from the docks,
a gaggle of girls buy ice-cream,
the dogs hang round gossiping
the road goes nowhere
and t wo old peolpe hold hands.

You know you're in Ullapool
when the little town is a proud town,
the steamer sails for Stornoway,
the shops are stowed with locals
all saying it is "quiet",
and a wifie on the sea-front
locks herself out of her car.

You know it is Ullapool
when everyone knows the poets,
when Inverness isn't mentioned,
when you can't find a policeman
but you couldn't possibly need one.
It is Ullapool
when you are as glad as this
you have been there today.

Oban, summer night

We were only there for an hour –
no plans to travel on
so strolled around the piers
where a train slept terminally
and the Mull steamer lay docked
as the smooth bay of the night
took its hot, short holiday from light

and recalled stories of the past:
of how the busker had stood up to the laird,
how all the seals would bob along the harbour,
and how three well-respected Gaelic poets
had walked into the Royal Bank of Scotland
sozzled, and ordered whisky ("Sorry, sir,
this is the Royal Bank of Scotland.")

The same old pubs with open doors and singing
spilt into the square, the quay, while boats
crept out on midnight trips around the bay,
a place to eat fish suppers in the presence
of old and unembittered seagulls. A town to keep
through years, though we won't stay away
so long this time, we said, and drove away.

Oakwood, Western sea-slope

this poem can begin and end anywhere:
it has continuous repeats.

salt shades, each one vulnerable.

And, so few yards away, the sea
batters the shell-grain sand;
bright gold, green lime, russet, tangerine

rounded on oak trunks, here marine
blues, deep dark variants, aquamarine's sheen
or turquoise cloud the glistening surf.

Oakwood climbs away, an old lichen
hanging on its oakboughs. Honey-scented,
thick yellow clotted honeysuckle,

rose and gold, sunsets behind branches
where mistletoe glints for the billhook.
Oak wears fresh foliage in old forks,

rosette with no explaining words,
steps into summershoals of acorn
salt shades, each one vulnerable.

And, so few yards away, the sea
batters the shell-grain sand;
bright gold, green lime, russet, tangerine

rounded on oak trunks, here marine
blues, deep dark variants, aquamarine's sheen
or turquoise cloud the glistening surf.

Oakwood climbs away, an old lichen
hanging on its oakboughs. Honey-scented,
thick yellow clotted honeysuckle,

rose and gold, sunsets behind branches
where mistletoe glints for the billhook.
Oak wears fresh foliage in old forks,

rosette with no explaining words,
steps into summershoals of acorn
salt shades, each one vulnerable.

The Ends of Roads

I love the ends of roads,
that peter out on proms,
circle round a teashop
closed half the year,
suddenly become private
where an old casement swings
or a jeep is parked,
turn into a dell, grassy
or a classy drive,
become "unsuitable
for motors" and for feet –
forever await a ferry
or fail below a mountain peak.

Then when the trail runs home,
and I have driven over
a fabric of fringed ends,
blind country crossroads
angled like a web
over hillocks and bays,
cul-de-sacs, farmsteads,
a gapped wall, a frail gate –
a slight hint of trespass
hidden and overgrown
in the bright, glinting lanes –
I love their misty range
and solitude on the journey –
yet always fnd them strange.